KU-739-712

Contents

Page

Weblink: www.curriculumvisions.com

Do we need electricity?

Electricity travels along wires and makes all kinds of things work.

We use electricity all the time. It would now be very difficult to live without it.

In the past people did live quite happily without electricity. It was only made useful about a hundred years ago. So what do we need electricity for, and why can't we do without it now?

Let's start by looking at what life was like before electricity.

This kitchen, and everything in it, belongs to a time (called Victorian times) over a hundred years ago. Everyone then lived in an age before electricity.

Royal Borough of Kingston Upon Thames

Using electricity

Pe... app

Curriculum Visions

Science@School

Teacher's Guide
There is a Teacher's Guide available
to accompany this book.

Dedicated Web Site
There is a wealth of supporting
material including videos and activities
available at the Professional Zone,
part of our dedicated web site:

www.CurriculumVisions.com

The Professional Zone
is a subscription zone.

A CVP Book.
First published in 2008

Copyright © 2008 Earthscape

Authors
Peter Riley, BSc, C Biol, MI Biol, PGCE,
and Brian Knapp, BSc, PhD

Senior Designer
Adele Humphries, BA, PGCE

Educational Consultant
Jan Smith (former Deputy Head of Wellfield School,
Burnley, Lancashire)

Editor
Gillian Gatehouse

Designed and produced by
EARTHSCAPE

Printed in China by
WKT Co., Ltd

Curriculum Visions Science@School
Volume 2F Using electricity
A CIP record for this book is available
from the British Library.

ISBN: 978 1 86214 264 0

Picture credits
All pictures are from the Earthscape and
ShutterStock collections.

This product is manufactured from sustainable
managed forests. For every tree cut down at least one
more is planted.

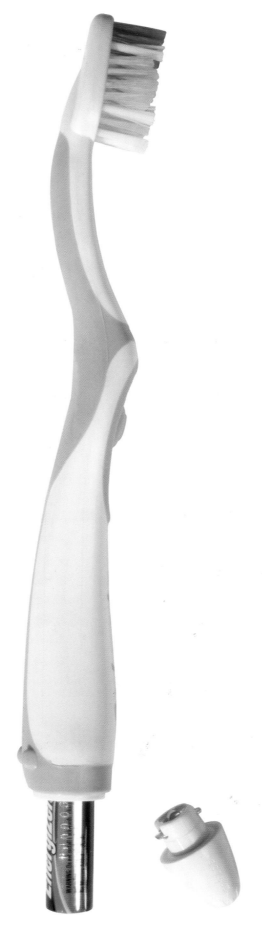

A battery-powered toothbrush.

You need electricity to make a birthday cake even if you cook by gas (the controls use electricity).

Surfboarding and all outdoor sports can still be done without electricity.

Electricity makes the petrol burn in car engines, powers the headlamps and works the stereo system.

We need electricity to get water – unless we are prepared to pump it for ourselves (the pumps in the waterworks run on electricity).

What electrical things would you see in a modern kitchen?

Weblink: www.curriculumvisions.com

Electricity and light

Electricity is easily changed into light.

One of the first uses of electricity was to make electric light. Lights are used in homes, offices, schools, streets and factories.

Cities use so much electricity for lighting that you can see them from space.

Traditional light bulbs get hot as well as giving out light. This wastes a lot of electricity. New energy-saving light bulbs are much better.

Traditional light bulbs.

Energy-saving light bulbs.

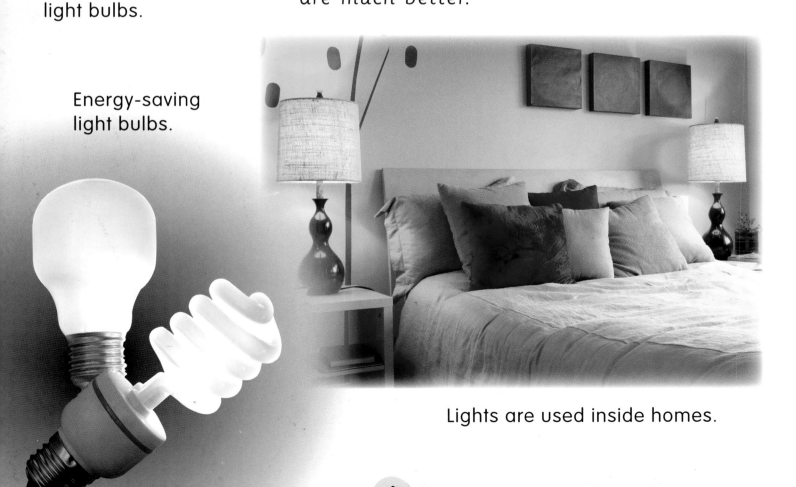

Lights are used inside homes.

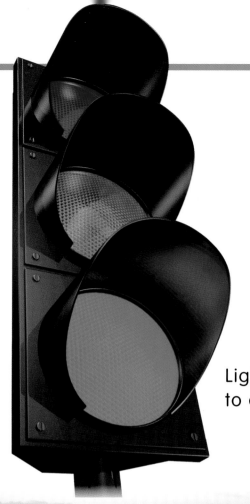

Televisions give out light. This is how we see the programmes.

Lights are used to control traffic.

This is New York City at night.

Do you use ordinary or energy-saving light bulbs at home?

Electricity and heat

Electricity can be used to make things hot. Here are some of them.

heating wires

Electricity normally flows in wires without making them hot. The cables to your computer don't get hot, do they?

However, special wire can be used that does get hot. The heat can be used for warming rooms, for ironing, for cooking and many other jobs.

Here is an electric stove. Inside each cooking plate there are heating wires.

Weblink: www.curriculumvisions.com

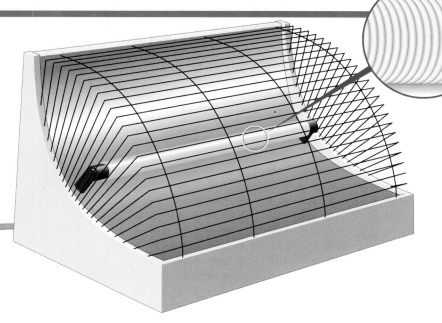

This is an electric fire. The heating wires are wrapped around a tube. The heater has a special guard so that no one can touch the wires by accident.

This is an iron. The heating wire heats up the metal bottom of the iron. When we push the iron over clothes, the hot metal plate heats the clothes and the fibres straighten out.

This is a kettle. The heating wires are in a special waterproof case.

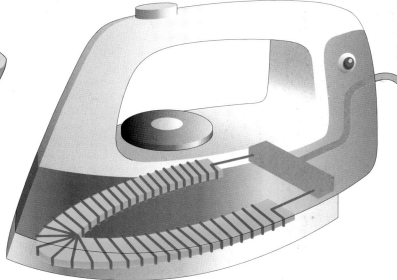

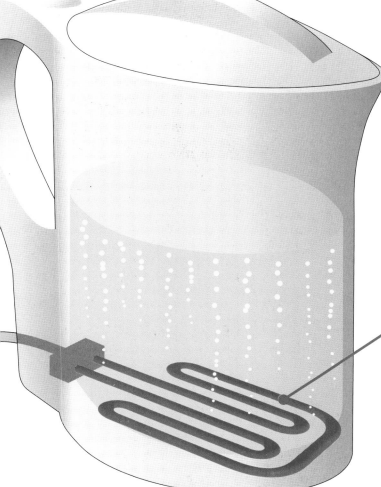

heating wires

Which of these is used in your home?

Weblink: www.curriculumvisions.com

4 Sound and movement

Electricity is used to make many things move. Some movements produce sounds.

Electricity is used to make lifts work, to power electric drills, to work lawnmowers and hedgetrimmers.

Inside all of these things are motors. Motors turn electricity into movement.

Electricity is also used to make movements in the air. These are sounds. The loudspeaker in your radio or CD-player changes electricity into sound.

The larger the sound, the more electricity is used. These headphones (above) use very little electricity. The loudspeakers (right) use a lot more.

Weblink: www.curriculumvisions.com

The escalators in this shopping centre have electric motors inside them.

These drills both use electric motors. The top one runs on batteries.

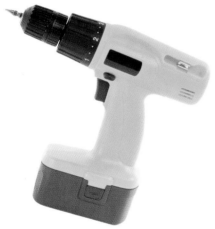

This is an electric hedgecutter. It uses a motor to work the blades.

This drill is connected to the mains by a lead.

How many things do you know that use electric motors?

Weblink: www.curriculumvisions.com

Mains electricity

Most things we use work with mains electricity.

Mains electricity comes to us from power stations. It is sent along thick cables strung on pylons, and then under the streets to our homes.

This kind of electricity is very powerful. It will run cookers and heaters and all of our lights.

Because it is so powerful we must never touch any mains wires or cables.

The cables carrying electricity under the streets are far bigger than those we have in our homes. Just look at the sizes!

home wires

cables under the street

How power is brought to our homes.

power station

How many things in your home use mains electricity? Use the picture above to help you to decide.

Electricity is brought under the street to the sockets in our homes. We plug computers and other mains equipment in to these sockets to make them work.

Cables on pylons carry electricity to homes.

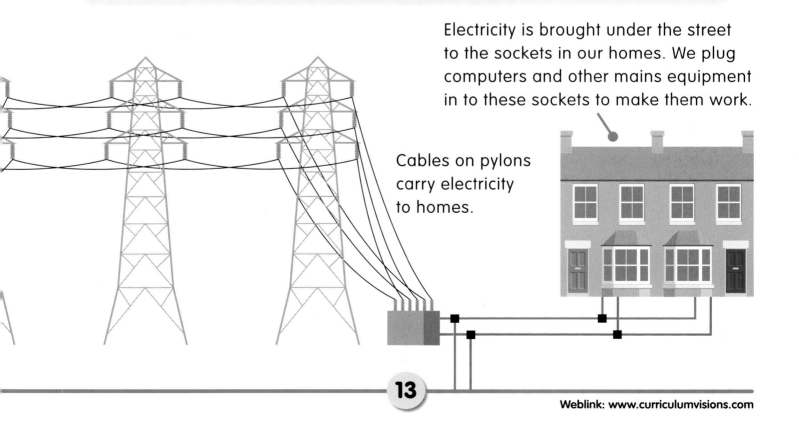

Weblink: www.curriculumvisions.com

6 Batteries

A battery can be carried about, and supplies us with electricity any time we need it.

Electricity from batteries is not as powerful as mains electricity. However, batteries can be carried about. You will find batteries in the remote controls for TVs and music centres, in torches and cameras, in music players and watches, in mobile phones and even in remote car keys.

Here are the batteries in a remote control.

There are many sizes and shapes of battery. Each does a different job.

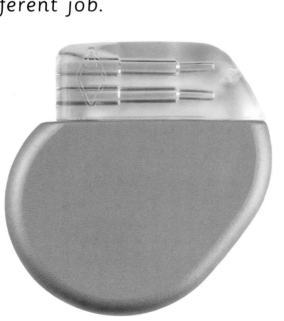

This is a pacemaker. It is used in people who have heart trouble. It is placed inside the body. Its job is to make sure that the heart works properly by giving it tiny electric shocks. It uses a long-lasting battery.

Weblink: www.curriculumvisions.com

This is a large battery used in a torch.

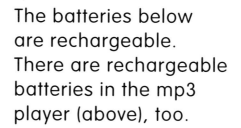

This is the small battery used in a watch and a travelling clock.

The batteries below are rechargeable. There are rechargeable batteries in the mp3 player (above), too.

This is a battery used in a camera.

What do you have that uses batteries?

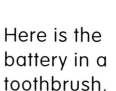

Here is the battery in a toothbrush.

Weblink: www.curriculumvisions.com

Looking inside a torch

A torch uses batteries and a light bulb.

Anything that joins electrical parts, such as batteries and bulbs, is called a circuit.

This is a torch. When you take it apart you find lots of things hidden inside the case.
All the things are joined to make a circuit. Make sure you can see each part.

1 There is a bulb, which gives out light.

2 There are two batteries.

3 There are some springs and holders.

4 There is a switch for turning the torch on and off.

What you might find inside a torch.

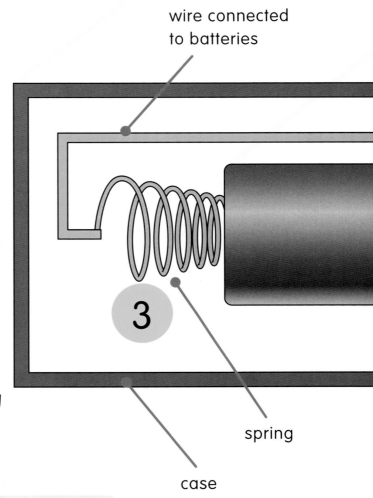

wire connected to batteries

spring

case

Can you take a torch apart and put it back together so that it still works?

Weblink: www.curriculumvisions.com

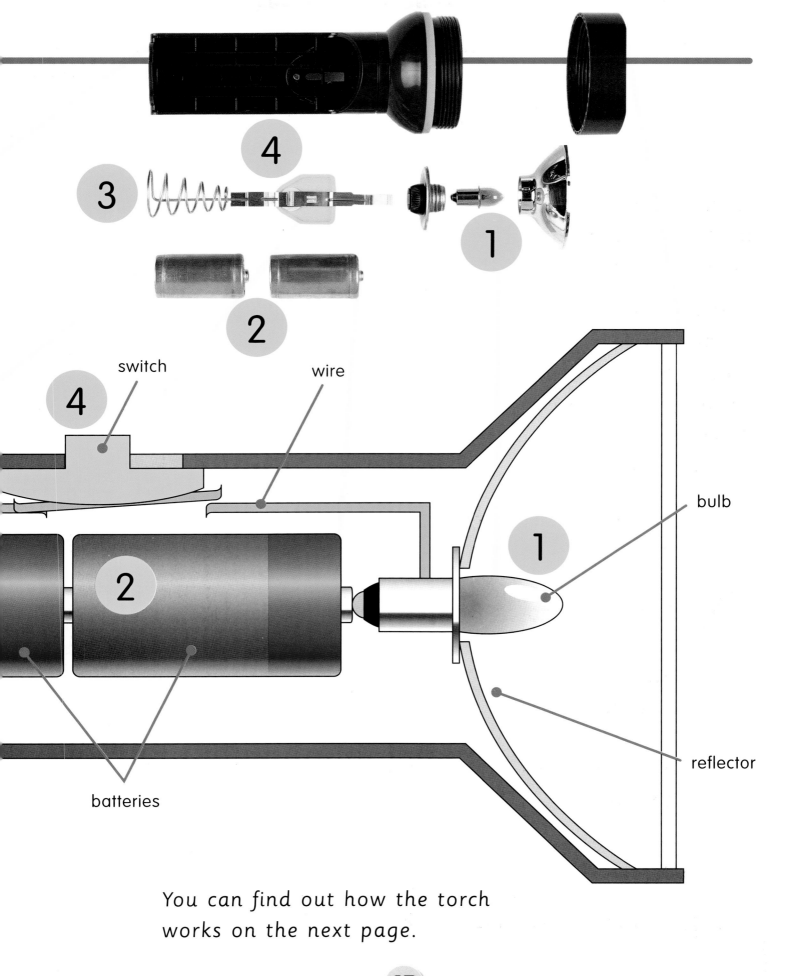

switch

wire

bulb

reflector

batteries

You can find out how the torch
works on the next page.

Making a circuit work

Electrical circuits work by making a loop. You must always make a loop or the circuit will not work.

A very simple circuit is made like the one shown here.

1 Connect a wire to one end of a battery.

2 Connect the wire to one side of the bulb.

3 Connect another wire to the other side of the bulb.

4 Connect the other end of that wire to the other end of the second battery. Make sure both batteries face the same way and that they are touching.

5 Make sure that all wires are firmly touching.

6 Double-check. Make sure the batteries, wires and bulb make a loop.

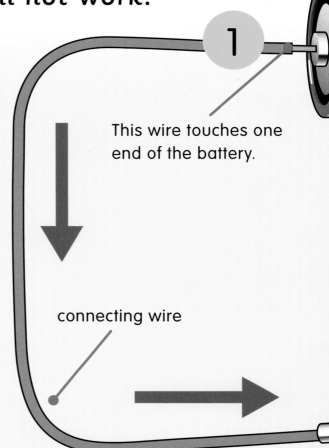

This wire touches one end of the battery.

connecting wire

How can you make the bulb go out?

Weblink: www.curriculumvisions.com

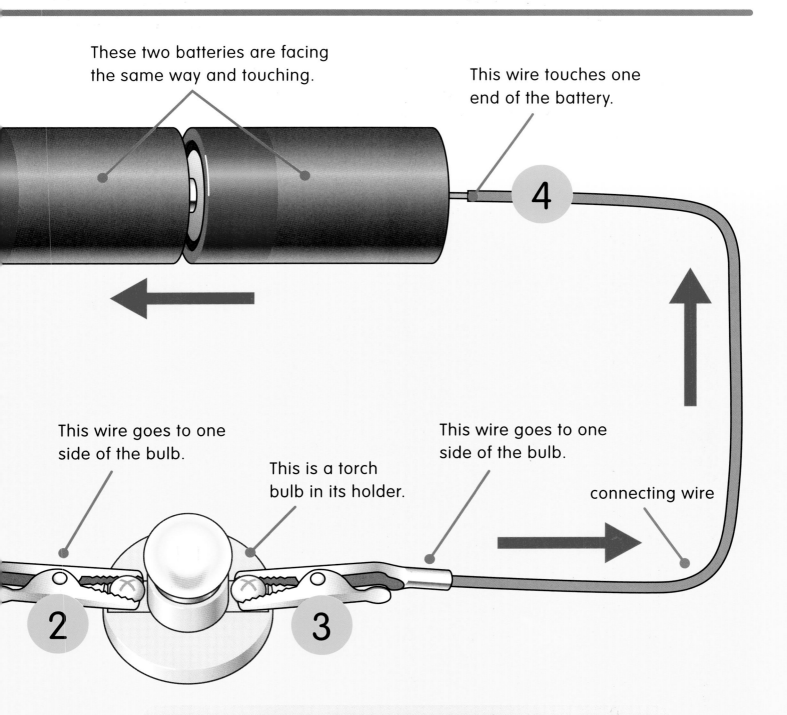

These two batteries are facing the same way and touching.

This wire touches one end of the battery.

4

This wire goes to one side of the bulb.

This is a torch bulb in its holder.

This wire goes to one side of the bulb.

connecting wire

2

3

This is what happens (follow the arrows)

Electricity flows from the end of one battery. It flows through the wire to the bulb. The electricity then returns to the end of the other battery and the bulb lights up.

Weblink: www.curriculumvisions.com

Circuits that don't work

Circuits need to be joined in a loop or they don't work.

Everything in a circuit has to be in a loop that starts at one end of a battery and finishes at the other end. Batteries always have to face the same way. Otherwise the circuit will not work.

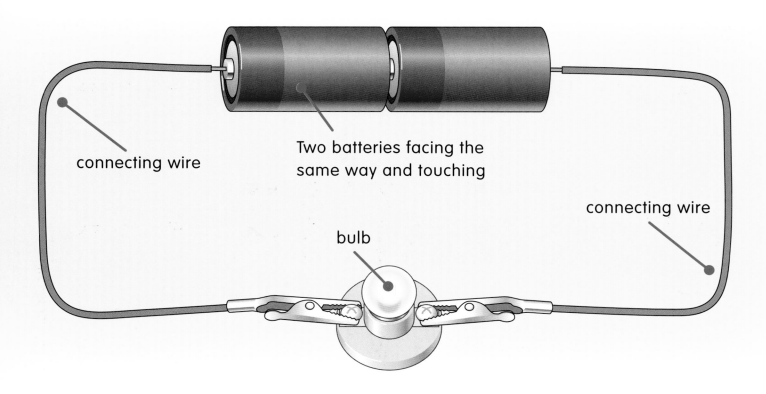

connecting wire

Two batteries facing the same way and touching

connecting wire

bulb

This circuit works and the lamp lights. Here is why:

1 Everything is in a loop.

2 The batteries face the same way.

3 The wires touch the batteries and the bulb.

Weblink: www.curriculumvisions.com

Non-working circuit 1.

Non-working circuit 2.

Why does the bulb not light in these two circuits?

Weblink: www.curriculumvisions.com

Words to learn

Cable

A thick wire, or group of wires, which carry large amounts of electricity.

Efficient

Does not waste electricity.

Electric shock

A sudden painful movement of part of the body when a current of electricity goes through it.

Lead (pronounced 'leed')

Wires covered in plastic, which connect plugs to things that use electricity.

mains lead

Mains electricity

Very powerful electricity, which can harm and kill people if it is not treated with care.

Plug

The connector at the end of a lead, which plugs in to a wall socket.

Power station

A large building where mains electricity is made.

Pylon

A large tower made of metal bars, which holds up electricity cables.

Socket

A place in a wall where a plug is pushed in so it can connect to mains electricity.

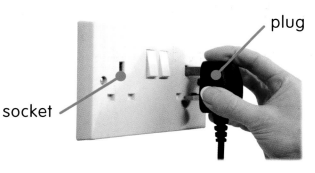

plug

socket

Weblink: www.curriculumvisions.com

Index

Weblink: www.curriculumvisions.com